Health & Wellness

More Than Your Workout

Deconstruct your cravings & wake up your body's natural weight loss system

Written by:
Stefanie Mori

More Than Your Workout: Deconstruct your cravings & wake up your body's natural weight loss system

Copyright © 2015 by Stefanie Mori

All rights reserved. No part of this book may be reproduced in any form or by any electronic or mechanical means, including information storage and retrieval systems, without permission in writing from the author. For information, contact Stefanie Mori at www.xohealthandwellness.com.

Use this for health related content:
The content of this book is for general instruction only. Each person's physical, emotional, and spiritual condition is unique. The instruction in this book is not intended to replace or interrupt the reader's relationship with a physician or other professional. Please consult your doctor for matters pertaining to your specific health and diet.

Use this for general:
All rights reserved. No part of this publication may be reproduced, distributed, or transmitted in any form or by any means, including photocopying, recording, or other electronic or mechanical methods, without the prior written permission of the publisher or author, except in the case of brief quotations embodied in critical reviews and certain other noncommercial uses permitted by copyright law. For permission requests, email the author at xohealthandwellness@gmail.com.

To contact the author, visit
www.xohealthandwellness.com

ISBN 978-1-944134-01-3

Printed in the United States of America

Table of Contents

Acknowledgments 5

Introduction 6
Back To Basics: You are all you allow yourself to be

Chapter 1: 15
You are what you eat - The food your body craves

Chapter 2: 26
Out of your office and into your life - The nourishment your soul craves

Chapter 3: 36
Step #1 - Out with the good and in with the great

Chapter 4: 41
Step #2 - Build your awareness

Chapter 5: 49
Step # 3 - Define your goals

Chapter 6: 55
Step #4 – Choose to put your health first

Chapter 7: 64
Stressed out - Silent cravings of chronic stress

Chapter 8: 68
Helpful tips to achieving health and wellness - Conquer your cravings

Conclusion 76

For my dad,

Giancarlo,

who showed me that love and intention could truly take you higher than you ever imagined you could go.

Acknowledgements

Institute for Integrative Nutrition
Thank you to the Institute for Integrative Nutrition, and to Joshua Rosenthal, for all you've taught me and for inspiring me to never stop learning more. Thank you for giving me the courage to live my authentic self and for all the love, beauty and awe that it has brought my life!

Rosemary Mangiardi
Thank you to Rosemary for her amazing inspiration, cleaver ideas, keen eye and support on this project! Your vision and PR mastery is unparalleled! Thank you for always sharing your gifts with me!

Amie Olson and Lindsey Smith
Thank you to Amie and Lindsey for their ongoing support and guidance throughout this process! Thank you for helping to turn a dream into a reality and for sharing your amazing gifts and talents with me! For continuing to remind me to have faith in the process and believe in all things possible, thank you!

Matthew
An extra special thank you to my amazing and incredible husband Matthew! For all your love, steadfast support, tenacious encouragement, and true wisdom, without which this book truly never would've made it to fruition, I thank you with all my heart! Thank you for embracing this crazy and wild journey with me baby! I wouldn't trade it for anything!

Thank you all for sharing your gifts with me so I could share this gift and my passion with the world!

With love and gratitude,
Stefanie

INTRODUCTION

Back To Basics:
You are all you allow yourself to be.

For many of us, when we wake up, what we think about first is generally NOT our health and well-being. We think about a long list of things, perhaps, about work, what we have to do as soon as we get into the office, what to wear to work that day, what to have for breakfast (some skip this step completely) and coffee, definitely coffee. We have moved so far away from putting our needs, and especially our health, at the forefront of our minds. That being said though, more and more, people seem to want to get back to a time when health was far less complicated, back to a time when we didn't need an alarm on a phone to tell us to take a break or leave work for the day.

If I know one thing about the co-relation between working hard and enjoying life, I know that looking after your health and well-being is pretty vital. The truth of the matter is that we all know this. But the question is why then do more of us not focus on putting our health and wellness needs first? Living a healthy life doesn't have to be complicated, but prioritizing your health and self-care is something that does require a call-to-action and something only you can choose to do. Without it you will only exhaust your resources and eventually burnout or worse. Through this book, I hope to share with you how very simple, fun and rewarding it can be to start putting your health first! I mean, who wouldn't like a little more "me" time in each day? If your main priority became to truly, whole-heartedly, take care of your health and well-being, what would the energy from that that allow you to do?

When your main priority is to take care of yourself, your needs and your well-being in life (not selfishly so, but in a way that empowers and excites you) you become able to eat beautiful food, be fitter and stronger, work smarter, faster, better, love deeper and achieve great things in the world. You already have a wealth of knowledge within you about what's healthy to eat and what's junk food, what you want and need to be happy and feel amazing. The key is to become more aware of these things and turn that knowledge into actionable next steps.

You truly are all you allow yourself to be. This book is designed to help you find and build awareness into your life and to create, for yourself, your own personalized stress management and self-care practices that will help you prioritize your health. This knowledge and awareness within your life will allow you to not only make healthier choices with the food you eat, but will also help you build healthier, stronger daily routines to see you through anything life throws your way, be it those demanding projects at work or that Suns-Out-Buns-Out Bikini Routine you keep meaning to get to. In the following pages I'm going to show you how to build awareness back into your life so you can tackle all of life's modern day challenges, start making healthier choices and develop empowering practices that finally work for you.

In my health coaching practice, I promise real results, which means I'm not going to tell you that in this book there's an easy solution to all your problems or that you can drop

10 pounds in 5 days. Nope, you won't find that here. Sorry. Everything you will learn in the following pages are tools designed to help you prioritize your health and self-care practices because I want the very best for you. When you decide to commit to your health and well-being, succeeding and thriving in your life become perks. Take a moment away from your busy schedule and sit with this book, be it an hour or a few minutes each day, whatever you can give to commit to the most important thing in your life: YOU!
By reading this book you are committing to:

- Deconstructing your cravings
- Losing weight naturally

But even more than that, what you're really committing to is:

- Your overall health and well-being
- Goals that are important to you
- Taking your life in a direction you want it to go
- Leading fulfilling, passionate and rewarding days

The perks of making your health and self-care a greater part of each day:
- Learning about the foods that truly rock and empower your body
- Losing weight naturally
- A healthier, fitter body
- A glowing, and radiant and clear complexion
- Less stress in each day
- More 'you' time
- Greater relaxation
- More love

Technology can be a great tool to use to help keep us on track with work and our fitness goals, but computers, the Internet, emails and apps aren't enough. I dare say with all that's written about health online, all the emails that bombard us at work and all the apps that are designed to help us track and tally our activities, our life is so busy spent trying to keep up with the health trends that we almost miss the point to stop and live our health goals. It's time to make a change to how we prioritize our health and well-being. This train of thought, along with a deep-seeded wish to bring people back to a healthy life that's simple, easy to follow and easily accessible, is what led me to write this book. How did our health and self-care go from being our most significant thought to being almost an afterthought? How did chronic stress and low energy levels become the accepted state of normalcy and how long can such a state last before chronic disease sets in? When did taking a vacation become so difficult for us as a society to do?

This got me thinking, what would it take for me, for anyone, to stop and become aware of how far removed we are from our health and well-being and what that does to how we live and perform in our lives? In considering these thoughts further, I concluded a simple premise that gave birth to the book you're holding: you are all you allow yourself to be. It really can be that simple.

Working hard is truly empowering (I love it), but, at the end of the day, if you're so exhausted, or worse sick, from stress, lack of nutritious food and staring at a screen all day that you can't even enjoy the fruits of your labour with those you love, then what's the point? I hope through this book to help you gain a sense of Personalized Health Awareness, which means prioritizing your health, knowing what you need to thrive on a personal level and gaining the ability to create self-care practices that work best for you. True health is more than just taking a pill and forgetting about the issue. Wellness begins from within. Your true health and well-being can be strong and long-lasting, but to get there you need to decide to make your health and well-being a priority and build self-care practices back into your life. You deserve to feel amazing by doing something special for yourself each day. By taking the simple steps outlined in this book you can create a healthy life that's flexible, fun and rewarding!

My goal has always been to make living a healthy lifestyle more accessible and something far more personalized than the one-size-fits-all mentality we so often read about today. This goal was born along my own journey, which, as fate would have it, began in the gym, working out. Growing up physically fit and petite my whole life, I knew instantly the moment weight snuck up on me and working out always seemed to me to be the simplest answer for how to get fit again. While I will always remain an advocate for leading a physically active lifestyle, a few years ago I found myself thinking: "What does one do when working out simply doesn't work anymore or maybe never has worked for you?" This line of questioning made me want to learn all I could about what makes our lives truly healthy. Through my journey of health knowledge & self-healing, I immersed myself in studying alongside the world's top health and wellness experts, learning numerous dietary theories, the art of deconstructing cravings, innovative coaching methods and practical lifestyle management techniques, becoming a Certified Health Coach in the process. Much to my surprise and excitement, I noticed the added bonus of losing those last unwanted pounds naturally along the way; weight that my intense workout routines never seemed able to make a dent in and which I couldn't figure out how to get rid of. As part of my own journey, I learned first hand how to maintain a healthy lifestyle while working in high stress jobs. If the journey that led me here has taught me anything it taught me that true health and wellness are so much more than just a workout. True health and wellness begin from within and losing weight naturally can be achieved without the expensive, one-size-fits-all diet, detox, pills or supplements.

I am so truly blessed that I am able to offer my clients support and guidance in achieving their health goals by creating a personalized program that's completely unique to their needs.

For more support, check out my 6-Month Program that will help you:

- Deconstruct your cravings
- Lose weight naturally
- Improve your energy levels and sleep
- Help you incorporate healthier food options into everyday life
- And much, much more!

I have included more details of my program later in this book.

More Than Your Work Out

♥ ♥ NOTES ♥ ♥

Stefanie Mori

NOTES

> "A JOURNEY OF 1000 MILES BEGINS WITH A SINGLE STEP"
>
> Lao Tzu

Chapter #1:

You are what you eat

You are what you eat. A simple enough idea that many of us have heard before, but have you ever really given it much thought? If what you eat fuels your cells to perform their roles, and they use that fuel to go forth and multiply, and all those little millions of cells are, in fact, you, then it's quite evident that you are what you eat. Now you might be thinking: "that's all well and good, but what does any of that have to do with my health?" That's a great question.

The premise is simple: The very food you choose to eat is what nourishes your body on a cellular level. You are what you eat. If you're eating food that's predominantly, or worse completely, made up of ingredients that are made by people in white coats (generally any ingredients we struggle to pronounce), which hold no real nutrient value, where is the body expected to get nutrients? When your body can't find nutrients, or fuel, from the food you're eating, then your cells and your body cannot possibly function properly. Cue disease and dietary disorders here.

Generally we don't think about our food and how it relates to our cells, but we should, at least on some level, recognize that the food we eat gives our cells fuel to function. If we're not giving our body the right food, perhaps we eat a lot of processed and refined pre-made foods, it's very hard for the body to function properly. This is how we are truly what we eat. All the nutrients we take in, all the food we eat, is what our body uses as fuel for cells. Arguably, the better nutrients we are able to give our body, the stronger our body becomes, the more capable our body is of building healthy cells, which keeps us healthier. This is, of course, a very simple explanation of the vast scientific processes occurring constantly in your body, keeping it thriving, and what we eat is only one component of our overall health and wellness. However, by looking more closely at how we are what we eat, one can't help but become more aware of the connection between the foods we eat and how our bodies react.

By becoming more aware of what you're actually eating, more aware of the ingredients that make up the foods you enjoy, you will notice trends in what you're eating. For example, if you notice that 16 out of the 20 things you ate in a single day had sugar in them, this could be good sign that you are eating way more sugar each day than you think you are, which could be a factor that is affecting your body and it's ability to shed unwanted weight. There are many other examples of this, but I think you get the idea. Many people have no clue what food makes its way into their body because they often aren't looking at the ingredients in the food they're buying. Or, for some of us, we try and diligently look at the ingredients in the food we buy, but then we eat out at lunch each day and have no clue what went into our food. When you aren't preparing the food you're eating, it becomes that much harder to control what goes into your food and into your body. Now don't go jumping to conclusions, I'm not saying that eating out is wrong and you should never eat out! Not at all! Eating out is amazing - I'm a foodie at heart so trust me, I get it! I love culinary experiences, but by being more aware of what's in the food I'm eating and the importance of giving my body good, nutrient-rich, clean foods, I can actively choose restaurants that value the quality of the food they serve. Making smarter food choices doesn't have to be complicated; it just requires a commitment to wanting to put your health first. While self-care begins within through our choice to commit to ourselves, one could say the next step is choosing to fuel your body with beautiful, nutritious, clean, and whole foods.

Get Cooking

When it comes to eating nutrient-rich food, knowing what's in your food is most important and there is no better way to learn more about that then to cook more of the food that you eat. Not only does cooking lead to learning what goes into certain dishes that you love, but it also means less chance for unwanted ingredients to slip onto your plate and into your body.

Cooking gives you control over what kind of food you put into your body, but, even more than that, cooking is a way for you to build a relationship with food and, eventually, build intention into the meals you so thoroughly enjoy. Cooking is one thing, building intention into your meals is an entirely greater process altogether. If you love to cook, then likely you already build intention into each meal you make simply by way of your passion. I have always loved working in the kitchen, cooking up a storm with my dad. Learning from him great recipes, neat tips and tricks and creating truly beautiful food to share with loved ones. I have my dad to thank for many things in my life, but most of all, for teaching me that real food bought with love and cooked with intention is beyond nourishing for the body, it nourishes our very soul. Intention in the food we prepare makes each meal nourishing for your body as well as for your heart and soul. In this sense cooking can be seen as a self-care practice if ever there was one. What's great is that you don't need to be a chef to put your heart into the food you cook, you just need to love your body enough to want to make great food for your health.

Putting together beautiful meals can be simple, easy and quick. There are so many amazing recipes online that are easy, delicious and a click away. Nowadays it's easier than ever. There are even some sites you can follow that are all about cooking with only a handful of ingredients, so it doesn't even have to cost you a fortune to cook good food for your body. If you don't have time to cook the majority of your meals, try starting small: make an effort to choose 2-3 days a week where you'll cook your meals and buying lunch only once a or twice a week. Not only will small changes like this be easier to maintain in the long run, they will also help save you money. Who doesn't like to save some extra money here and there? Choosing to bring your own lunch from home even just 3 days a week could save you upwards of $1500 a year! The main point is, whether you're cooking up a feast for friends and family or dining out, just be sure to be aware of what you're eating, and be committed to choosing more nutrient-rich options to fuel your body.

Beautiful clean whole foods, basically any food free from artificial substances and additives, are key ingredients to building a beautiful, healthy body. As often as you can, choose to eat whole foods, which are natural and simple for your body to recognize as real food. When in doubt, try focusing on food that's made with all natural clean ingredients. The more of whole foods fill your diet the less room there is for junk foods to find their way onto your plate and into your body. This is not a new premise by any means. It's written about and published everywhere you look. We all know whole foods in their natural form are nutrient rich and great choices for nurturing and strengthening the body. We've all read about avoiding food with pesticides, preservatives and additives and the benefits of choosing clean eating habits. Yet still obesity remains a severe global issue and chronic disease continues to rise up more and more, everywhere we look and in all age groups. With all the health and wellness knowledge at our fingertips you would imagine our world would be healthier. The premise remains true, you are all you allow yourself to be, which is only too true when it comes to the food you choose to eat. By choosing to add, for example, more leafy greens, fresh fruit and other local vegetables into your weekly routines and you are making the quality of your food count and making what you eat a priority.

When you think about it, the food we eat really does say a lot about our character, how we view ourselves and the opinions we hold around health and wellness. Although cravings are not the topic of this chapter, I think it important in discussing awareness around the food we eat to note that the food we crave speaks volumes about what's going on within our bodies. It's an empowering exercise to question why you might be craving certain foods at certain times during the day, or even whether stress might be playing a role. A great tip to help conquer cravings: whenever I feel I'm craving a treat, before giving into that craving, I drink either 1 – 2 glasses of water, or have a cup of tea, I often find this derails my craving. If I'm still craving the treat afterwards, I'll opt for a healthy snack option like almonds or a smoothie. By becoming more aware of what you eat and when you eat you can slowly begin to see trends in your eating pattern. This sense of self-awareness will help you better manage your cravings and help you understand why you have those cravings in the first place.

To Do List:

- 💜 Make a list of what you eat each day for a week and connect with what you're eating. Highlight any food you would like to make an active effort to remove from your day-to-day diet.
- 💜 *Helpful Tip: take this list with you when you go shopping as a reminder of what to avoid buying and putting in your pantry.
- 💜 Start cooking more meals. Look up at least 4 meals you have really wanted to try and pick 2, or 3 even, that you are going to commit to make this week.
- 💜 Pick a day to go shopping for the ingredients you'll need for this week's recipes and a separate day specially for cooking. Write these 2 special days down in your calendar. This will help ensure you cook the food you bought and save you money by not throwing away food that's spoiled before you remember its sitting in your fridge. Remember: it might feel at first like cooking is taking up more of your time, but it gets easier and you will feel amazing and empowered eating healthier, cleaner and delicious foods made by you.

Stefanie Mori

A Short Aside:
Meditation:
It's Not For Everyone, and That's Alright:

Not everyone is a fan of meditating and that's OK. Not everyone has patience for it or any interest in deep breathing. Then there are some people who love the deep breathing, but prefer self-guided meditations. Whatever your preference, I have found that in today's bustling world meditation can serve a great purpose in its ability to slow us down, even for just a few moments, in a day otherwise without pause. By slowing down and pausing for a moment you get a chance for some true 'you' time, which can be incredibly relaxing. One of my most favorite meditations is a tea meditation. If you've never tried a tea meditation, I highly recommend it. There are many ways one can perform a tea meditation. Below is what I like to do.

Tea Meditation

A tea meditation is a great form of meditation that you can virtually perform anywhere, even at work or on your commute home. It's simple, easy and a great way to build relaxation into your day, especially while on the go.

- Brew a pot of hot water while humming a happy tune.
- Choose a delicious tea to enjoy.
- While your tea steeps, take a few long, deep, breaths
- Once your cup of tea is brewed and ready, sit quietly with your cup of tea.
- When at a safe temperature, hold the cup of tea in both hands and feel the warmth of the tea.
- Let it warm you and comfort you.
- How does the tea smell?
- Take a deep breath and enjoy the soothing aroma of your cup of tea.

- Let it calm and comfort you.
- Enjoy a sip of your beautiful tea and let it warm you, soothe you and comfort you from within.
- Take another deep breath to soak in the warmth of your cup, the soothing aroma of your tea and all the pleasure it has brought you.
- Notice the calmness that it has bestowed upon you in perhaps an otherwise hectic day.

The More Modern Meditation Method

- Turn off your device and embrace your life.
- Take a long, deep, calming breath and pause for a moment in your day.
- This is some well-earned 'you' time.
- In this moment, breathe in gratitude for your life, your well-being and all the beauty bestowed upon you each day.

More Than Your Work Out

♥ ♥ NOTES ♥ ♥

Stefanie Mori

Chapter 2:

Out of your office and into your life

Reconnect with your heart and your health and life will follow.

Inspired beauty can be found in all things great and small. Inspired beauty is everywhere around us. What inspires you? What are you grateful for? What do you love? Perhaps it's going to the beach or heading out of the city and embracing the countryside. Maybe it's shopping for shoes, a new outfit or new accessories. Maybe it's something as simple as enjoying a picnic with a loved one. Whatever it may be, inspired beauty in the world is unique and personal to you, it's what holds true meaning for you.

Inspiration is a simple way to help you connect with what you're most passionate about; what your soul truly craves. Reconnecting with your heart can help build awareness of what's truly most important to you in your life. By building this awareness of what you hold closest to your heart you are able to connect with your authentic self. Simply surrounding yourself with what you love each day, you can become inspired. Adding inspired beauty into your life not only helps make you more aware, but it nourishes your soul, which is such an easy step to take towards furthering your awareness of your health and state of well-being. By building this awareness and connecting with your authentic self, it becomes almost effortless to create personalized self-practices that finally work for you and help you work towards a healthier life. Whether it's losing weight naturally, avoiding toxic relationships, learning how to really de-stress, or simply having some 'you' time each day, reconnecting with your heart and nurturing your soul through something as simple as inspiration gives you a clear connection with your authentic self, which ultimately helps you clearly identify your health goals.

This leads me to the next chapter.

The pages that follow here, and similar ones throughout this book, are designed to help inspire and strengthen your days. May they inspire you to reconnect with your heart and find what nourishes your soul.

More Than Your Work Out

♥ ♥ NOTES ♥ ♥

NOTES

IF LIFE IS A JOURNEY AND NOT A DESTINATION, THEN BE LESS FIXATED ON THE PURSUIT OF HAPPINESS, AND MORE FOCUSED ON THE HAPPINESS THAT LIFE'S PURSUITS BRING YOU.

Stefanie Mori

Sometimes the greatest risk we will ever take is being our authentic self.
Only by becoming our authentic selves can we truly reach our life's greatest potential.

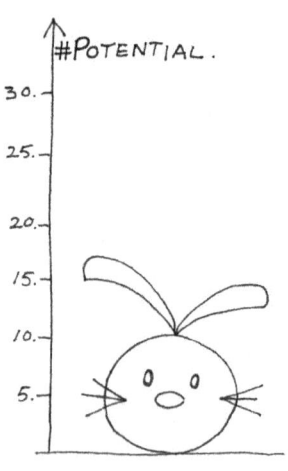

Stefanie Mori

More Than Your Work Out

Turn the discomfort of fear and the weight of doubt into the elation of excitement and the freedom of belief.

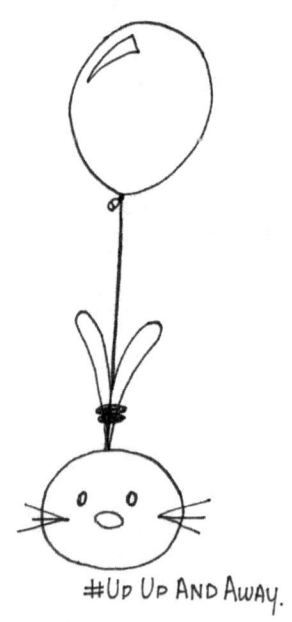

#Up Up And Away.

Stefanie Mori

Chapter 3:

***Step #1** - Out with the good and in with the great*

The following are 4 simple steps that are designed to help you build awareness and bring inspiration back into your life. By becoming more aware and in tune with your authentic needs you will be able to envision true goals for a healthier life and create a wealth of self-care practices that you can actually feel add value to your life. These self-care practices are unique to you, your needs and your goals, working to get you to a healthier life in a way that's flexible, fun and rewarding. Through these 4 simple steps you are committing to making your health and well-being a priority and to living BIG.

Step #1 - Wake Up: Out with the good and in with the great!

Perform the following series of steps somewhere quiet where you will be un-interrupted. You will also need a note pad or piece of paper for this exercise.

- Take a moment and breath, take an extra deep breath, feel the stress of needing to be in a hurry leave your body. Continue deep breathing until you no longer feel rushed.

- When you finally feel the world around you become quiet and still, then you're in a great place. Stop and stay here in this space for a moment.

- In this place of relaxation and calm, see your life as it is right now. What does it look like to you? Note down any areas you want to improve on, no matter how small. This exercise will allow you to more clearly define your goals and what matters most to you in your life.

- Take another deep breath, feel good knowing that you've taken the first simple step on your journey towards living a life that you feel great about, and smile.

- Breathe deeply once more, this time recognize your breath filling your lungs and raising you up. Remind yourself in this moment that you deserve to feel great; that you deserve to be healthy and happy and that you are all you allow yourself to be.

To Do List:

♥ Stop for a moment in your day and make a list of things you are grateful for in your life.

♥ Write a list of areas in your life you would like to improve on and goals you would like to achieve.

More Than Your Work Out

NOTES

NOTES

> "When you talk, you are only repeating what you already know. But if you listen, you may learn something new."
>
> Dalai Lama

Chapter 4:

Step #2 - *Build your awareness*

This step is all about building true awareness into your life. With greater awareness you become more self-centered, meaning you become more focused on who you really are and what matters most to you. It's about reconnecting with your authentic self and remembering how important it is to your true health and well-being that you give your body and soul what they need to flourish. We are, after all, at our core, spiritual beings in a material world. Learning what your body and soul need to flourish is a huge step towards helping you create stronger, more personalized self-care practices, and even greater stress management. By building awareness into your life you become more able to see yourself authentically and much more capable of identifying the stresses that you choose to allow into your life. When you can identify what causes you stress, you'll be able to see it coming a mile away and choose to build self-care practices into your day that help counter-act that stress. What's even better is, that by noticing where stress creeps into your life, you'll be that much more prepared to deflate unforeseen stress that comes your way.

Step #2 – Build Awareness:

- Treat yourself to a nice latte or cup of tea and sit quietly. Put your phone away where you can't hear or feel it, or better yet turn it off completely. Think of all the things you simply love, things that make your world truly amazing.

- Make a list of all those things that you absolutely love. Write down at least 10 points.
- Read back over this list and feel good about yourself and all the beauty in the world. Breathe deeply in this moment and feel gratitude for all you love.
- On a fresh piece of paper, think about all the beautiful food you enjoy eating throughout the week, Monday to Friday, and write it down.
- Read back over the list of food you enjoy eating and highlight everything that includes a whole food, like a stir-fry for example.
- *Remember, a whole food is food that genuinely exists without artificial substances and is free from additives.

Once you've completed this exercise, ake note how much of your daily diet includes whole foods and what else your eating. What kinds of foods didn't you highlight? Become more aware of what you're eating. Prepare healthier food options ahead of time to add more nutritious foods into your weekly routine. I always like having one day set aside each week for preparing healthy options, but depending on my schedule sometimes I opt for 2 prep days. This is a great way to help you stay on track, especially when you're busy and on the go a lot.

Make an effort to build awareness into your life, especially around what you love most and what food you're eating. This is a fun and easy way for you to connect with what makes you happiest, what you love most, with the food you're actually eating and with your authentic self. When you're able to really connect with your authentic self you will be in a great place to know what you need more of in your life and what you don't, which will help you create solid self-care and stress management practices that really work for you.

To Do List:

- Build awareness into your life around two key areas, what you love most in the world and the food you enjoy eating.

- Post these lists up next to the mirror in the bathroom or somewhere else you will see them often each day and let them serve as reminders for you to connect with yourself, your needs and what matters most to you.

- Review the list you made Chapter 1 of the food you eat in a week and those key foods you want to remove from your diet. Post a copy of this list up where you will see it each day as well, perhaps next to your bathroom mirror or on the fridge.

- This coming week make an effort to really think about what you're eating and craving and try preparing fresh fruits and vegetables to add into your weekly meal plans.

More Than Your Work Out

♥ ♥ NOTES ♥ ♥

NOTES

You cannot achieve greatness as long as you're unwilling to accept your authentic self.
It is only through your authentic self that greatness has a voice to be heard.

Chapter 5:

Step # 3 - Define your goals

Step #3: Defining Your Goals and Setting Your Sights

Connecting with your authentic self is like a breath of fresh air; it feels freeing and simply amazing! If you're not ready to connect with your authentic self, that's OK too! Connecting with what you love most and with the food you give your body from the previous step, are both great tools to use to help you better know your true self. From this place of love and awareness you can define greater direction in your life by creating a list of goals that bring you happiness and fulfillment.

Start with where you are:

- Make a list of your goals. List as many as you feel you would like to focus your attention on. Think quality not quantity here. The goals you set should be ones that you are most able to start working on from where you are. This will improve your chances of success. As you achieve the goals on your list, you can always revisit this step and build more challenging goals for yourself. Having a list of goals is so helpful and writing them down really helps get you from where you are, to where you want to be. Being aware of your goals and what you most want to work towards achieving, especially when it comes to your

health goals, is vitally important nowadays more than ever. Our lives have gotten so noisy and crowded with everyone else's thoughts and directions; it can be easy to get sidetracked by all the chatter.
- Sit quietly somewhere, perhaps with a relaxing cup of coffee or tea, and review your list of goals.
- What do you want your health to be, and how do you want to feel?

To Do List:

- What do you want your life to really look and be like?
- Post your list of current goals somewhere you will see it daily. Each time you see it, be sure to read through and remind yourself of your goals. This is a great way to check in with yourself and ensure that your goals are being met.

More Than Your Work Out

❤ ❤ NOTES ❤ ❤

Never let anyone tell you not to set your sights high and aim for the stars. That's their fear talking! Not yours!

#Aim For The Stars.

Chapter 6:

***Step #4** – Choose to put your health first*

Step #4: Choose to put your health first

What you choose to allow your health to be is completely up to you. If you want to prioritize your health and get to a stronger place of happiness, wellness, and strength you can choose to do so. By becoming more aware in all aspects of your life you can better connect with your authentic self, your needs and goals in this life. Above all else, your main job should be to take care of yourself. You need to choose to make your health a priority. Ignoring or pushing aside your health and well-being will only result in you becoming more tired and defeated.

Start each day thinking about what matters most to you, not checking your emails. Your health will thank you!

When I wake up in the morning, I can often hear the birds singing to their hearts content, greeting the day with purpose and what sounds to me like a whole lot of joy. Whenever I hear this, I just lie there and share in the joyful sound! Such simplicity. Nature is a great inspiration. Even on the rainy days inspiration can be found, while lying in bed listening to the rain come down. I will often lie in bed or get ready and think to myself, what makes me healthy. Sometimes it's the smoothie I'm going to have for breakfast or the workout I'm going to accomplish, but it's also thinking about all the love and happiness in my life. Spending time each morning thinking about what matters most to you means you're that much less likely to reach for your phone first. I'm not saying that checking emails or your social media is bad. Not by any means. I just know that, like breakfast for your body, the first "meal" or nourishment you give your heart and soul each day is vitally important to the kind of day you can have.

Next time when you wake up, before you reach for your phone to check emails, or before the thoughts of work and pressing to-dos run away with you, before you simply get up and rush off to your day, give yourself a moment of your time, even just 1 minute, which is such a small part of the day ahead. Take this small moment and lie in bed, breathe deeply to help you relax and recognize a sense of calm in your body. If you don't feel calm, perhaps your thoughts are already running away with your day, just continue to breathe deeply until you feel more relaxed. Being able to relax in these moments generally shouldn't be too hard, but if it takes you a bit of time at first, that's OK too. We're all different. I promise the reward of greeting your days with your heart is well worth the effort. Take a deep breath!

In this moment just listen, take another deep breath and greet each day with all your love and gratitude. Think of what you love and all you're thankful for.

As you get up to start your day, continue for a while to think about what you're most grateful for. As you get ready think about what you love the most and let it make you smile and feel good inside! Starting each day in this positive and love-filled way is such a powerful thing you can do to set up your health for the day. In this powerfully positive state of mind, your body receives specific messages from the brain and releases endorphins and feel-good hormones, like oxytocin, which can change even the way your body receives the food you eat. This is a much more complex topic than I have room to delve into here, but my point is that taking time each morning for yourself, to building awareness and intention into how you start the day, is just one small way of choosing to put your health first.

More Than Your Work Out

TO DO LIST:

♥ Start by spending your weekend mornings practicing a soul-nourishing routine.

♥ Incorporate small powerful, positive and soul nourishing practices into your weekday mornings.

♥ Tips to help you create soul-nourishing, morning routine practices:

- Set your alarm 30 minutes earlier. Getting up 20-30 minutes earlier can give you the time needed to enjoy a piece of your morning for yourself, especially during the week.

- Perform deep stretching and/or a yoga flow session to help wake up your body.

- Meditating can also be a really relaxing and rewarding way to begin the day. Lie in bed or sit with your morning cup of tea or coffee and enjoy sitting quietly for a moment while thinking of nothing but what you're most grateful for.

- Drink a tall glass of water with lemon and help wake up your metabolism.

- Play your favorite feel-good playlist to get you going in the mornings. This is a great way to help get you up, moving and feeling amazing.

- If you are fortunate to have your bedroom near a large enough window, leave your blinds turned down a bit at night so that your body naturally wakes with the daylight.

- Enjoy a sit-down breakfast. If you must take a breakfast to go, prepare all the pieces the night before, take your breakfast with you to go and give yourself a little time when you arrive at your destination to enjoy breakfast. Remember: the value of eating slowly and enjoying your food will help fill you up longer and help keep you from overeating or snacking uncontrollably later.

Aside:
Finding your palm tree

I love the saying "Find your palm tree"! This is such a simple way of saying find what matters most to you in your life and surround yourself with that each and every day. It so perfectly summarizes what we're all really trying to do in this life, which is find a happy place to call home. And by "home" please know that I don't mean where you reside, your place of residence or your address. I mean that place of pure bliss that brings you, your heart and soul, nourishment and nothing but big smiles, warm feelings and the utmost joy and pleasure. When I embarked on this journey to become a health coach I did so with the most heart-felt, deep-seeded notion that living a healthy life didn't have to be complicated and that I could work hard and live big without sacrificing my health to do so. Finding your palm tree isn't meant to be something you dream about all your life and never achieve or enjoy, nor is it meant to be only something you get to enjoy in your years of retirement. Such a beautiful state of being – pure bliss (however it appears to you) – especially with all our hectic schedules should be lived throughout every day and shared with loved ones every chance we get. I assure you this premise is not too good to be true, nor is it a pipe dream, but it definitely is the road less travelled and for some of us that will always be a deal breaker. However, for all those bold, beautiful and classy adventurers out there, think of life as more then a measure of how many un-opened emails you have in your inbox, or the kind of car you drive, but rather a great journey you want to be healthy enough to enjoy. On your road to finding your palm tree, first and foremost you need to prioritize your health.

TO DO LIST:

 Find your palm tree

How To Find Your Palm Tree:

- Find whatever inspires you, whatever makes you smile, glitter and glow from within and surround yourself with that. The happiness you feel in this moment is something you deserve to feel each and every day. This exercise is designed to help slow your thoughts and focus your attention inwards to hear the whispers of your soul.

- Continue to nurture your heart and soul and you will have opened the door in your life to allowing wellness in.

More Than Your Work Out

♥ ♥ NOTES ♥ ♥

Chapter 7:
Stressed Out

Is stress draining your energy? Could stress be causing you to overeat or crave junk food? Is stress causing you to gain unwanted weight? Who can't relate to the affects of stress on some level?

As stress is such a prominent factor in everyone's lives these days (isn't chronic stress the new norm?), I felt it only right to include a more specific section on the importance of learning how to manage the stress in life. Stress exists for everyone, but it shouldn't control you or your life and it definitely shouldn't be making you sick. If you feel that stress causes a chain reaction of any kind, then it's probably safe to say that you need more or stronger stress management practices in your life. By a chain reaction I mean stress causing a lack of eating all day, which causes binge eating at night, or perhaps a lack of sleep from stress (even subconscious stress), which leads to drinking double-shot Americanos and sodas all day and continuing not to sleep well. Chronic stress has many forms that look different for each of us, which makes it hard to spot, but the key is you need to protect your body from stress. I think stress is one of the most dangerous conditions in our lives today. Not only is it a natural part of each of our days, but it's something many of us have never learned to protect ourselves from. It's not an issue many people are talked to about. That being said though, to simplify an extremely detailed process, when stressed your body will release certain hormones, which are designed to help you flee in a stressful situation. The body is trying to protect you from whatever is causing you stress/fear. However, because much of our stress today is invited in, so to speak, these hormones aren't used for running away or fleeing as they once were, instead they can often cause unwanted responses in the body such as inflammation and weight gain. This book is not designed to delve into the scientific details of hormonal responses in the body, but if you've never heard of Cortisol, I encourage you to do some research into what kind of hormone it is and how it can affect your body. Knowing more about how your body functions, even if just on a hormonal level, and what causes certain reactions within the body, will help you deconstruct cravings, even some you never knew you had, and increase your self-awareness dramatically. This will greatly improve your ability to make healthier, more educated choices, including choosing when and how to melt stress away.

TO DO LIST:

♥ Think about how stress affects your life. What are some areas of your life that would be improved if stress wasn't a factor? What are some things in your life that you feel stress is making worse?

More Than Your Work Out

NOTES

Chapter 8:

Helpful tips to achieving health and wellness

Scheduling time for yourself

It's just like scheduling an appointment for work. Put an appointment in your calendar to meet yourself somewhere. Be it at a yoga class, the spa or gym, even a bubble bath at 9:30 p.m., whatever it may be; be sure to schedule true 'you' time and be there for yourself. This is how you incorporate self-care and stress management practices into a hectic weekly schedule. Put it in the calendar! Trust me, if you don't, it becomes too easy to completely overfill your schedule and never get that time you deserve! This might seem tedious at first, but it really works. Not only does putting it in your calendar make you feel more accountable, it also blocks out the time you need to give yourself. Stick to the appointment you've committed to yourself, it's as important, if not more, than any other major appointment you make, like the doctor, or dentist.

YOU are all you allow yourself to be. Give yourself the attention you deserve and start living a life you feel loved and fulfilled by. It really is that simple.

Relax and Melt Your Stress Away

When it comes to creating solid stress management practices that fit into your life, you need to focus on what you find most relaxing and do what works best for you. It's similar to the saying "one person's food is another person's poison". As with all self-care practices, it's vitally important that you create relaxing stress management practices that work with your needs, your goals and your schedule. Feel free to get ideas and pull inspiration from a wide variety of health and wellness sources, and share your practices with others, but always be sure to remain aware of what your needs are and what will work best for you.

Here are some examples of stress management practices that I've created in my life that I think you might enjoy as well:

Bubble Baths

Drawing a bubbly, warm bath filled with your favorite relaxing aroma and soapy suds can be a great way to unwind, especially after a long day at work, an exerting workout routine or yoga class, or even just as a great way to get ready for bed. If you're looking for an ultra-relaxing experience, why not try an XO Premium Bubble Bath – a bubble bath with class!

XO Premium Bubble Bath Recipe
A relaxing way to unwind and sooth your soul

Ingredients you'll need:
- Favorite scented bubble bath soap

- ½ cup of Epsom salts
- 1 tsp. of baking soda
- Aromatherapy bath or body massage oils
- Additional options include: candles, background music or ocean soundscape, and/or a nice glass of wine or cup of tea.

Steps

1. Draw a nice warm, soothing bath and add the bubble bath soap (for best results soap that gets extra bubbly), Epsom salts, baking soda and any oils you wish to use. For aromatherapy massage oils, I recommend visiting your local health or whole food store and asking if they carry all natural bath and massage oils.

2. While your bath is filling, you can add ambient music or place and light several candles on a ledge of your bathtub.

3. Just before hopping in, put your phone on silent and anywhere other than the bathroom, pour a glass of wine or cup of tea to enjoy with your relaxing XO Premium Bubble Bath and dip in to soak in the suds for some quality YOU time.

*Please note that all ingredients listed above are suggestions that work best for me. The exact quantities used and/or duration of how long you spend in the bath should be decided by you, based on your own personal preference.

Relaxing Footbath

Another great option to help relieve the body's overexertion, tension and stiffness is to try a relaxing footbath. This is especially a great option for when you know you have a busy week at work, or perhaps will be travelling a lot, and are short on time. Footbaths provide a lot of the relaxing benefits of a full XO Premium Bubble Bath, but I find they come in handy when you haven't got much time, like when you're on the road, travelling. Since you will only be soaking your feet, you can use the same materials as you would for your XO Premium Bubble Bath, just simply lower the volume because you won't need to use as much water, and follow the same steps. It is so relaxing and soothing to the soul!

A beautiful dinner for two

Prepare a beautiful dinner for 1, 2 or more, with all the trimmings

What you'll need:
- Placemats
- Plates and utensils
- Napkins
- Wine glasses, or other fancy glassware
- Candles
- A beautiful DIY centerpiece

This is designed to be a romantic dinner for two, but it can just as easily be a fun festive dinner for friends. You could even make a fun girl's night out of it! Prepare your favorite dish and serve one of your favorite drinks.

If you need a hand, incorporate meal prep as part of the event and invite your date or friends over ahead of time to help you chop, peel and prepare all the goodies. Working in the kitchen with loved ones and friends while enjoying delicious drinks, and appetizers maybe, can be thoroughly enjoyable and connects you to food in an entirely more intimate way. Plus, enjoying a meal you love with people you love makes for truly memorable moments.

Whatever your form of relaxation, just be sure to be aware enough to incorporate these practices into your busy schedule. Remember it's all about creating self-care and stress management practices that work for YOU! Write all your self-care practices into your schedule as you would an important meeting for work. Before you know it, coming up with fun, flexible and rewarding ways to take care of your health and well-being will become a staple in your prep-night practices. Be sure to stay true to your authentic self, your needs and your goals. Self-care is one of the best things you can do to give your health the attention it deserves. Don't wait for someone to give you the time you need to take care of yourself, take the time you need to look after your health and well-being and allow yourself to truly thrive!

TO DO LIST:

- Carve out set time each day to devote to your self-care practices. Write these times into your calendar as important appointments.
- Choose 1 or 2 relaxation practices to incorporate into your weekly schedule.

What works best for you? Create 2 or 3 relaxing stress management practices that you can do today to help relax your body and nourish your soul. Use the time you scheduled to try different self-care practices to find what works best for you with your schedule and lifestyle.

More Than Your Work Out

♥ ♥ NOTES ♥ ♥

Conclusion

Creating a healthy life and why there's no app for that

There is a huge deprivation of self-care that many of us are affected by in our lives, be it a lack of human interaction, a lack of physical contact, contact with nature, a lack of nutrient-rich food or a lack of physical activity. Creating a healthy life starts with the commitment to making health and wellness a priority and grows by implementing flexible, fun and rewarding self-care practices. By creating your own unique and personalized self-care practices you are helping to improve your chances of success in creating a healthy life. We all know what foods are healthy and which aren't. There is an abundance of health and wellness materials online that anyone can look up at any time. The issue is that despite all the knowledge, no one acts on it. By becoming more aware, I hope to encourage action. I call you to invest in your health and well-being and that of your loved ones. Choose to be well. You are all you allow yourself to be.

While apps are great and can hold you accountable and tell you how many steps you've taken, or calories eaten, only you can find gratitude and awareness in caring for your health, your body and your life. A lot of Apps share information with you and help you in your fitness goals, they track and measure progress, but they can't tell you if you're on the right track for your health and well-being. The four simple steps I have presented to you here are small steps you can take with you, starting right now. You can share them with loved ones and friends! Being healthy, beautiful, glowing and passionate about life isn't unattainable, it doesn't have to be complicated or come at a steep price. We ourselves choose to make it so.

Remember, creating great things like a healthy beautiful body and a life full of love, passion and wellness, isn't a quick fix you will find wrapped in a pill. It's an exhilarating journey unique to all of us and one worth taking. Wellness comes from within, first and foremost, and only you can decide to commit to making your health and well-being a priority. There's no app that can do that for you. A healthier, happier lifestyle doesn't have to be complicated. It requires commitment to small changes and awareness to make healthier choices. I believe that life was meant to be passionately lived and thoroughly enjoyed! As my dad would often say, "Buon appetito"!

Support that's more than just a book!

You've read the book, now connect with me online for more health resources!

My Program: More Than Your Workout

In my 6-Month More Than Your Workout Program I guide and support clients in achieving their health goals by creating a personalized program that is unique to their needs. When was the last time you received the personal attention you deserved and really talked with someone about your health? Whether you're goal is to manage your cravings, lose weight or simply learn to cook healthier meals at home for you and family, I'm here to support you to achieve the health goals that matter most to you.

Connect with me and learn more about the programs I offer at
www.xohealthandwellness.com

Sign up to receive my Monthly Newsletter!
Not another email blast! If you're like me, then the last thing you need are more time-wasting emails flooding your inbox! I offer a newsletter published once a month and am passionately committed to putting together hand-crafted, carefully selected content that is reliable, relatable, and value-driven, full of health and wellness tips to save you time and money, self-care practices, delicious, fresh, seasonally-inspired recipes, and much more! Best of all, flexible enough for all schedules.

Sign up at www.xohealthandwellness.com!

Connect with me on Facebook
www.facebook.com/xohealthandwellness

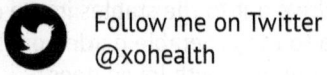
Follow me on Twitter
@xohealth

I'm also available for workshop and speaking engagements, as well as Market Tours and Pantry Makeovers. Contact me at xohealthandwellness@gmail.com for more information.

About Stefanie Mori

Through her perseverance to redefine her own health and wellness and heal her body, Stefanie immersed herself in studying alongside the world's top health and wellness experts, learning numerous dietary theories, innovative coaching methods and practical lifestyle management techniques, becoming a Certified Health Coach in the process. Through XO Health & Wellness, Stefanie passionately shares her knowledge and supports and guides her clients through personalized programs that help them develop and create a happier, healthier life in a way that's fun, flexible and rewarding. She is driven to see her clients succeed and excel in achieving their health goals and loves seeing them thrive in their lives. Stefanie currently lives in North Vancouver, British Columbia with her loving and supportive husband, Matthew. When she's not seeing clients, hosting a seminar or reading up on current health trends, she can be found with her husband relaxing in the mountains, taking a drive out to the stables in the country, enjoying a workout, tending to the vegetable garden or simply just cooking and enjoying beautiful food with loved ones.

Because living a health lifestyle shouldn't have to be complicated!

Connect with Stefanie for a free health consultation at
xohealthandwellness@gmail.com
and visit www.xohealthandwellness.com
to download your free cleanse cheat sheet.

www.ingramcontent.com/pod-product-compliance
Lightning Source LLC
Chambersburg PA
CBHW070655050426
42451CB00008B/357